GW00372876

Your Life

An Introductory Guide To Writing Life Stories

ANNA FOSTER

YouByYou Books

ISBN 0 9550235 0 5

Set in Book Antiqua 11pt
Swallow illustration © Mike Langman
Illustrations reproduced with the kind permission of the author's family
Printed by the Friary Press, Dorchester

YouByYou Books,
Swallow Court,
Dashmonden Lane,
Biddenden,
Kent TN27 8BD.
Tel: 01580 291965
Email: info@youbyyou.co.uk
Website: *www.youbyyou.co.uk*

This book contains general advice and guidance and no responsibility can be accepted for loss or expense incurred as a result of statements in this book. Laws change and readers should check the current state of the law where it applies.

Contents

Introduction	**7**
1. Why Do You Want to Write a Life Story?	**10**
Leaving a Legacy	10
As Catharsis	11
As a Present	11
Collective Memoirs	11
A Pictorial Record	12
A Contemporary Memoir	12
2. Your Audience	**14**
3. Collect Your Source Material	**16**
4. Setting Out a Structure	**20**
Chronological	20
Big Bang	21
Thematic	21
Diary	22
External Events	22
Benefits	23
5. Starting to Write	**25**
Style	25
Tools for Writing	27
How to Start	28
Do's and Don'ts	31
Ghostwriters	32
6. Writing as a Routine	**33**
Length	34
Appearance	35
Setbacks	36

Losing Motivation	36
Difficult Subjects	37
7. More Techniques	**39**
Quotes and Extracts	39
Speech and Visual Breaks	39
Chapter Headings	40
Introduction	41
Dedication	42
Family Tree	42
Appendices and Bibliography	42
Index	43
8. Collective Memoirs	**45**
9. Editing Your Manuscript	**48**
Style and Content	49
Shape	50
10. A Good-Looking Book	**51**
Formats	51
Covers	53
Paper	55
Text	55
Pictures	56
Captions	57
Pictorial Record	58
11. Publishing and Printing Options	**66**
Printing and Binding	67
Self-Publishing	67
Cost	68
Number of Copies	68
12. Should I Sell My Book?	**70**
ISBN number	70
Audiences	70
Price	72
Bibliography and addresses	**73**
Author Biography	**74**

— THE BRIDAL PARTY.—

BACK
Tommy , Flo. (my father), Emmie Ted. Mr.Spanton   Tim.
        (Myself) Bride.   (Mother)   Mrs. & McSavage .MissHedley.
Nellie   Annie   Isabel   Ben.   Miss Spanton

The Choral Society was still rehears-
ing, when we arrived and Mrs. Eccles,
wife of our popular doctor came out at
that moment. I hastened to introduce
my bride oblivious that it was too dark
in the unlit street, to successfully introduce persons. But what proud groom
would think of this!
        I had rented the two best rooms —
a sitting-room and a bedroom in my old
lodgings, and my bride was well received
by Mrs. Wilson and they came to an a-
greement over the cooking facilities.

A page from a hand-written memoir, started in 1936. Albert Copps's *Reminiscences*, written for his family, is now being read by his great-grandchildren. His account of his own wedding makes a fascinating contrast to the ceremonies his descendants know today

To my parents

Introduction

A long time ago my mother asked me to write a memoir of my father. He had led an active life in Tunbridge Wells, setting up and running local charities. Although I made some notes, I never wrote the book, always begging the excuse of too much work. I regret that I never completed the task which would have captured life in post-war Britain, with its idealistic social care system, and also our family life in Kent. Most of all, it would have given my children the opportunity to read about the grandfather they never knew.

Years later, a friend was researching a post-graduate thesis in Berlin about German children from mixed ethnic backgrounds. These were extraordinary stories from otherwise ordinary people. My friend mentioned that she had met a writer who specialised in people's life stories.

My mother's words came back to me and I realised that there might be people who would like to write such a book, but who, rather like me with my father, always found reasons for putting it to one side. 'Can't write, won't write,' seemed to sum up such an attitude. Yet, the desire to leave a record of ourselves runs deep, ever more so as we get older, and I found that people were enthusiastic about writing a memoir, but felt that they lacked the necessary skills and needed encouragement.

So I began to help people write their life stories. Sometimes I give advice about writing the manuscript itself, sometimes I help to turn the words into a book. It is a thoroughly rewarding activity; authors have become friends, and indeed, some of my friends have now become authors.

From the experience of helping other people to write their stories I have drawn up this introductory guide. Whether you are recently retired and looking for a project, have returned from gap-year travels, or wish to write up someone else's story, this book is for you.

You may consider yourself too 'ordinary' to be the book's subject, but you are of great interest to your family and friends. To future generations your life will seem fascinating, not least for its domestic detail. Anecdotes about the washing machine breaking down and using a microwave for the first time will place your life in a historical context. The Channel 4 programmes, *The 1900 House* and *The 1940s House*, intrigued us with their tales of the domestic daily grind.

More recently, the BBC series *Who Do You Think You Are?* traced the ancestry of well known TV figures like Ian Hislop and Moira Stewart. But what do we know of our own great-grandparents' lives?

You may wish to record the changes which you have witnessed in your lifetime. The increase in travel and the growth of entertainment, in particular the birth of television, mean that you have experienced more of the world than any previous generation. Your impressions of countries barely developed by tourism, and your responses to the media age, will be interesting to future generations who will take these things for granted. And it also gives you plenty to write about.

You don't need to be a literary genius to write a book. If you can write an email or a letter you will be able to write your memoirs. This book gives you helpful suggestions about writing and suggests material to include in your book. You will draw inspiration from diaries, photographs and newspaper cuttings, and you can recount your stories in the same chatty style in which you normally write.

Information is also included about making the best use of

your photographs and illustrations. Pictures will bring your book alive and there may be some 'readers' who only look at the pictures and barely read the text.

You may wish to have your book bound as a hardback or a paperback, but it is equally acceptable to put some typed sheets into a ring binder. If you want to mark a birthday or anniversary with your book then you may choose a more stylish presentation. Advice and some idea of cost is given for different formats. I have also included a section on selling your book, although I would exercise caution in committing your own money when you have no idea if your book is commercially viable. On the other hand you may decide that you can sell a few copies locally which merits some expenditure.

Most importantly, writing your life story should be enjoyable. Put a few words down on paper. Share the experience and let others read your book as you write it. Let your life tell its own story.

***

I have received invaluable help in writing this book. First, I'd like to thank the authors with whom I've worked over the last few years. Their experiences have enabled me to produce this guide. Thank you to Joan Bower for reading the manuscript and for bringing her sensitive insights to bear. And thanks to Joan, Jane Pendered and Bill McMillan for allowing me to reproduce material from their respective books. Finally, Alan, my husband, provided endless encouragement and cast a professional eye over the finished article. Thank you to him and my family for their love and support.

1. Why Do You Want to Write a Life Story?

Writing the story of your life is rather like having a photograph taken. It provides family and friends with a record - or a snapshot - of you. You have an opportunity to leave the story of how you would like to be remembered. Future generations can also enjoy the private biography of a family member who they never knew, and will get a picture of the times in which you lived.

You may decide to write a life story for a variety of reasons - it's important for you to understand your motives because they will determine the style in which you write.

Here are some reasons why people write their memoirs.

Leaving a record for children and grandchildren
This is probably the most popular reason for writing a life story. You may wish to write about your own life, or that of your partner or parent.

The desire to leave a legacy and to pass on memories of family events is strong. The fact that your own life may be 'ordinary' makes it no less interesting to the next generation.

Perhaps the subject of the book (it may be you) has experienced an 'extraordinary' event, like a war, or has performed a valuable service for the local community, and you wish to provide an accurate account of this. In this case, your book may be of interest to a wider audience than your family and friends.

If your motivation for writing is to leave a family record you will want to include as many anecdotes and stories as possible.

Your family will be less interested in facts they can find in a history book and more eager for details about aunts, uncles, early homes and, of course, your antics and misdemeanours. You're going to have to dig deep into the memory bank.

As catharsis

Writing can be a comfort and release if the subject about which you wish to write has had an emotional impact on your life. Such subjects could include the death of someone in the family or a breakdown. Therapy often provides a means for coming to terms with difficult events and, as part of therapy, 'writing out' the emotion can help you to distance yourself from the pain. You may not find the courage to write until years after the events have happened.

This may be coupled with the hope that by writing about your experience you will help others to cope in a similar situation. It's also a way of thanking people who gave you help at a difficult time in your life.

As a present

For those of us with an interesting member of the family, the offer to write up their life story as a present, is doubly rewarding. Perhaps a parent, or great-uncle, has achieved much in their life, but is unwilling to pick up the pen themselves. He or she might be too infirm to undertake such a project. By offering to hold the reins, be involved with the project, and even pay for the publication, you might provide the necessary motivation. The time spent together, looking at old photographs and sorting through letters, is also a pleasure in itself.

Collective memoirs

A book which records the achievements of a group of people is an excellent way of marking an anniversary. Such organisations might include an amateur dramatics society or a local history society. One group marked the Millennium by producing a book of their two-mile lane, including the histories of the houses and the lives of the present residents (see opposite).

You might be drawn together by an event, such as the D-Day Anniversary in 2004 which prompted many war-time memories. The BBC's D-Day website attracted 60,000 such recollections.

You could also compile a collective memoir of someone who has died, with recollections from family and friends.

A pictorial record

Your life story is probably going to contain many pictures. The growth of digital printing technology means that you can include as many photographs as you like without adding to the cost. You could decide to make these pictures the focal point of your book if they are of sufficiently good quality. As the saying goes: 'A picture's worth a thousand words'. In this instance you could save yourself writing several thousand words by concentrating on the pictures. Your final book may resemble a photograph album rather than a written life story, so think carefully if this is the right option for you. In Chapter 10 there is a section on producing a pictorial record.

A contemporary memoir

A life story need not span a whole life or be told by someone when they reach their later years. A twenty-something who has just returned from an unusual gap-year experience might write an account of their adventures. If you are about to head off on such a trip remember to take a diary.

The recovery of a young person from a serious illness, such as a child from leukaemia, would also provide a very moving record. A parent or close family friend would need to help a child write such a book.

If you work in a profession with a short lifespan, such as sport, dance or music, then you would probably write your life story as your career starts to wane, in your thirties or forties. Even if you are not a famous celebrity you may be well-known locally and within your field. You may be able to commentate intelligently about your sport or profession, while 'celebrity' writers might concentrate more on lifestyle and their moments of heroism.

Moat Lane, Cowden/ Chiddingstone Hoath in Kent

an update to celebrate the year 2000 AD

This book aims to provide a picture of Moat Lane at the turn of the year 1999/2000, with notes taken from recollections and records touching on some aspects of life in the lane earlier in the 20th Century. Whilst the aim of the contributors has been accuracy, no claims are made on this score. Neither is it claimed to be a complete history of the lane but is aimed to be a snapshot of the lane as it is, with brief historical notes.

Although the main text deals with properties fronting onto Moat Lane, as defined by postal district and electoral register, there are also references to properties and people on the fringe, where these are relevant.

We are indebted to the following for historical information and pictures: Edenbridge and District Historical Society, Betty Strudwick of The Moat, Parish Councillor Margaret Bond, St Andrews Convent, Edenbridge, Courier Newspapers of Tunbridge Wells, Topham Picturepoint of Mark Beech, Pinewood Studios Stills Library and to the residents of the lane for their cooperation and contributions.

W. McMillan
June 2000

Bill McMillan's book about the lane where he and his family live in Kent. In the short introduction to this collective memoir he explains his motives

2. Your Audience

While you think about your motives for writing a book you should also consider your intended audience. Most life stories are written in the first instance for family and friends. They will want to read a book which captures *you*. Some of the facts in the book may well be familiar to them - weddings, births etc - so they will want to hear your slant on them. They will be fascinated to read about aspects of you with which they are not familiar. Incidents from childhood, early schooldays and first loves, are riveting material for people who met you subsequent to these events.

You may wish to record information which is sensitive to individuals. Think very carefully about the impact of what you write on your audience. Where there has been a family tragedy or divorce, imagine the reactions of your readers. You may cause hurt or upset - and decide that this is unavoidable - but at least be aware of the nature of the material in your hands.

Very occasionally, a person may decide that he or she does not want their book to be read until after their death. Perhaps they feel this is the only way to reveal an old affair or a love-child. If you are considering a book to break the news about a secret part of your life be particularly sensitive about the effect this will have on the individuals concerned. You won't be there to answer their questions.

Beyond your immediate circle your audience may well extend to the local community or to a specialist group of people. Such stories might be about someone who has died or who has a long-term illness in which case the audience would include carers, fellow sufferers, help groups and local people who know or knew the individual. Or it might be a story about a retired diplomat or serviceman, in which case colleagues or fellow officers will be interested. You may decide to write a more formal life story, with fewer tales about home life, but more anecdotes and stories relating to your career and colleagues.

If you intend your book to be read by a wider audience still, maybe you should seek a commercial publisher. Much of the advice here will still be relevant when it comes to the techniques of writing, but don't part with your own cash if a publisher is prepared to. In the first instance, it is probably worth writing a synopsis of your intended book, and possibly a sample chapter, and consulting *The Writers' and Artists' Yearbook* for appropriate publishers and further guidance.

Vanity publishing is when the author pays for the publication of a book in order to sell it. You should only resort to doing this if you can't find a commercial publisher and are fully aware of the potential for financial loss.

Your Life is about self-publishing, in other words it helps people write their memoirs for family and friends. It doesn't tell you how to produce a commercial winner. This makes your book no less valid, it just means that you have chosen to write a life story, in the same way that others might have a portrait painted.

3. Collect Your Source Material

Before you start to write or even structure your book look at the material from which you will take your inspiration. It's time to dig out boxes of old photographs and search through cupboards for your diaries and notebooks.

Here is a list of the different kinds of source material which you will find useful:-

Letters and postcards

Letters you receive become your property. Might you wish to quote from them? Even though you are entitled to do so without permission, it's diplomatic to get the sender's approval. Equally, if you wish to quote from a letter which you have sent, you'll need the permission of the recipient.

Diaries and notebooks

Take your time to read these carefully as they could be one of your main sources of material. Make a note of important entries and earmark any sections which you could quote in full.

Household accounts

These can provide snapshots of expenditure and can place your life story in a social context. How much was a quarterly fuel bill in 1950, for example, compared to today?

Photographs

Take great care when looking at photographs, not just at the content of the picture but at its quality, because these pictures are likely to provide the illustration for your book. At this point, use the pictures as inspiration to jog your memory about events and places, and jot down your recollections. Don't worry about placing them in chronological order, as you may later decide to group your pictures differently. If there are any pictures missing of significant members of the family, see if you can track them down by writing to other family members.

School reports

These can often be very amusing for readers as they learn that Uncle Ted hated rugby or that Auntie Pauline was always getting the giggles.

You can either quote from a school report or, better still, use one as an illustration.

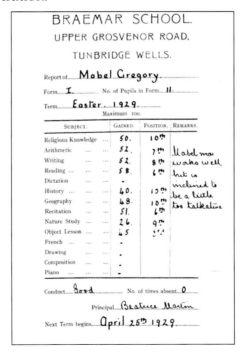

Birth and death announcements
Make sure that you get important dates right.

Scrapbooks
A very useful source of poems, drawings, newspaper articles, achievements at school and at work.

A family tree
You may find that research into a family tree goes hand-in-hand with writing a life story. The two subjects certainly overlap. It is very informative for readers if you can reproduce a family tree, as it gives all the key dates and people at a glance, and saves you repeating explanations in the text. Even if you don't already have a family tree it is invaluable to draw up your own simplified version, showing your own generation and one either side of it. Place it near the front of the book for easy reference.

Fitting together the pieces of the jigsaw: Gordon and his RAF records

The internet

This is an invaluable resource if you have lost touch with someone. You might be able to find them through a website like *www.friendsreunited.co.uk*, or by looking for their name on a search engine like Google. If the person has a profession or trade they might have their own website.

It's unlikely that all these documents will have been kept in an ordered pile, so take your time to locate and look through them. Coming across old photographs and rereading diaries can be one of the most pleasurable aspects of writing a life story. Don't rush this process because as you sift through everything ideas for the book will come to you.

Sit down with a pen and notepad at your side. To start with, make a list of your different source materials. Then under each heading note down individual documents, letters and diary entries you wish to include. This will provide a useful checklist once you have begun writing.

Keep the items you intend to use in an accessible place. For example, when you have read through all the letters keep the ones from which you wish to quote and put the rest away. Otherwise your living room may start to be overrun by the project.

On the other hand, don't let this research period become a throwing-away exercise. Don't be tempted to discard anything which might be useful later.

Other source material may come from family members or friends. Write to people at an early stage as they may take a while to find the articles themselves.

4. Setting Out a Structure

I t's very easy to 'start at the very beginning, a very good place to start', as Julie Andrews would say in *The Sound of Music*. But most professional writers, whether they are attempting an article, short story, or longer book, map out a structure of their work, before they begin their manuscript. By giving your book a shape at this very early stage you will get an idea of its length, how long it will take you to write, and whether you need additional material.

Chronological structure

A life story, by virtue of its subject matter, may be written chronologically. In this case, write out possible chapters on a sheet of paper, along the following lines:

Birth and Parents
Early Years
School and Teenage Years
First Job
First Love
Meeting a Partner/Marriage
Children
Career
Middle Age
Retirement

The milestones in your life may vary considerably from these, so choose appropriate chapters.

These are very simple headings (and not final chapter headings, just guidelines). Against each one write down key words and phrases. So, against Early Years you might note: moved house, relationship with grandfather, good/naughty child, stories about you at this time (which your parents told you subsequently), birth of a sibling and so forth. You can add to this list at any time.

Big bang structure
You don't have to tell your story chronologically, however. There may be an incident or period in your life which stands out and has provided the catalyst for you to write the book in the first place.

For example, if you have excelled at a profession or hobby you will want to devote a greater part of your book to this subject. If you are a keen ornithologist, say, you could start your book with the highlight of your twitching career, describing the surroundings and the bird in some detail, including your own excitement and feelings at this moment. The second chapter could place this experience in the context of your hobby, and not until the third chapter would you start to review other areas of your life. Remember to include dates so that the book still has a timeframe.

This kind of structure works when a dramatic incident forms the cornerstone of the book, such as an illness, a breakdown or a great achievement. You immediately draw the reader in, so that he or she is 'hooked', and then subsequent chapters provide the background to the incident, or continue the story.

Thematic structure
This might suit the record of a diplomatic career. You could order the material by location for example, especially if your postings were diverse. Your book is likely to contain many anec-

dotes, often relating to local places and people, and you could make your observations of cultural diversity the main theme.

Diary format

If you've kept a regular diary then you could choose to structure your book as a diary. After all, you've written it once, why write it all over again! Even so, you will probably need to edit your diaries, maybe quite substantially, to reduce them to a readable length. You can leave out less interesting entries. It is best to keep the diaries in chronological order and add any explanatory narrative as necessary. Make sure that your original diaries contain enough action or description to keep the reader's attention. Because the format itself is repetitive the reader can get bored or tired of having to 'start again' with each new entry. The flow or pace of the book needs to be sustained.

External events structure

Another method is to set your own story against events taking place in the outside world. This can be particularly helpful if you have forgotten the detail of a certain period. For readers it can also help to place your life story in context. Otherwise you might seem to be living inside a bubble.

The Queen's Golden Jubilee in 2002 drew up to one million people to London. What were you doing during the Silver Jubilee in 1977? Remember Concorde?

For this exercise you need two columns, one for historical events and one for you. Let's take the 1960s:-

My Life	Historical Events
1960 At school	*Lady Chatterley's Lover* court case
1962 Go to Glasgow University	Cuban Missile Crisis
1963 At university	Beatles' first LP *Please Please Me*
1964 Spend summer in Greece and Italy	President Kennedy assassinated
1965 Graduate. Study for post-graduate teacher training certificate	
1966 Unemployed	
1967 First job in a secondary school	
1968 Teaching	Prague Spring, Czechoslovakia
1969 Go to Woodstock Festival in the US	Woodstock Festival

It's become something of a cliché but you could recount what you were doing on the day Kennedy was assassinated. You could also see how your life fits in with trends at the time. Were you part of the 'Swinging Sixties' or did that era not appeal to you?

Outside events add colour and perspective to your tale. If possible, include a photograph of yourself present at a historical event, such as one of the Jubilee celebrations.

Benefits of a structure

One advantage of a structure is that it will provide you with discipline once you start writing. If you find that you're getting bogged down in one particular chapter, you can stand back, remind yourself of the original structure, and see where you're going wrong. Equally, if you get writer's block, you can stop writing, look at your structure, and find the inspiration to switch to a different section. After a break, you may find it easier to return to the difficult chapter. It's like having an architect's drawing in front of you.

A structure isn't set in stone. It is a tool to help you with the writing process. Additional material may come to light as you write, or you may have forgotten or lost other material - both could mean that chapters have to be added or taken away.

Chapters can be as long or as short as you like. They should be used to mark the staging posts of your life, and give the reader natural breaks. Look at some books you have enjoyed reading and note the length of the chapters.

You can rework your structure during the writing process. If you really grind to a halt or get 'waffle-itis' it might be a good idea to discuss the problem with a partner or friend and see if they can help you get back on course. You could also seek advice from a professional editor.

Once you have your structure mapped out you are ready to start writing.

5. Starting to Write

Writing is a very individual process. To some it comes easily, to others it can feel laboured and unnatural. If you enjoy writing, and do so on a regular basis, then you will probably start a life story with ease. However, you may need extra help to get going and below are some suggestions.

Do you have a style?
To readers, the word 'style' means that the voice they hear in the book is yours. They will recognise you not just from the events which you recount but the way in which you tell the story. The closest you come to this normally is in letter-writing. When you write a letter to a relative or friend you have an audience in mind - them. They are now the audience for your book and, without addressing them directly, you can start to write as if you were recounting an event to them in a letter. Always write about yourself in the first person, as this sounds natural. Here's an example of how a letter to a relative can be tweaked to become part of your book.

Dear Susie,

I had to write and let you know that young Jamie rode so well in the gymkhana. I was as nervous as ever - I couldn't watch at some points! - but your niece kept her cool, even over the biggest jumps, and had a clear round. We'd been up since 5.30am, getting Starlight ready, and drove through pouring rain for two hours. At the ground, there were horses and riders everywhere, and we had to wait until midday for Jamie's class. Both horse and rider kept calm, which was remark-

able, as Jamie knew that if she did well we had promised her a new pony for Christmas. It's just so expensive, keeping up this hobby of hers.... I blame you...

And in the book,

From an early age our daughter Jamie had shown considerable promise at riding, which I think she must have inherited from my sister Susie, because I was always very nervous around horses. This must date back to my childhood when both my sister and I rode, but after I fell and broke my collarbone I never fully regained my confidence. However, I didn't want to let that hinder Jamie and, although we could ill-afford it, we encouraged Jamie to ride, so much so that she became 'pony-mad'. I remember one gymkhana when she still had her first pony Starlight; we drove through the pouring rain for what seemed like hours. The showground was muddy and overrun with riders and horses, but my daughter showed her customary cool and performed well, no doubt motivated by the thought of a new pony for Christmas. Looking back, I can see how riding gave Jamie a lot of self-confidence.

Both pieces of writing convey the facts, the emotions of the mother and the contrasting behaviour of the daughter. But the second piece of writing fills in the necessary background information and gives a retrospective viewpoint. In both pieces of writing the 'voice' is the same, it's just that in the book the mother has learned, over time, to express her emotions more objectively than when she wrote to her sister immediately after the event.

Find your own voice

Letter-writing has further uses. Take the time to reread some letters and look at how you write when you are not putting too much thought into it. Are your sentences long or short? Do you describe places imaginatively or do you content yourself with 'the view was beautiful'? Try to analyse your own writing. Do you hold back on your emotions in letters? Or do you spend pages revealing how you feel about someone or an event? There are no rights and wrongs here as to how you *should* write, it's just an attempt to get to know your own writing better. By listening to your own 'voice' in a letter you will get a better understanding of how others will react to you in the book.

You can analyse your diaries in the same way. Of course the audience was different here - you. But you may find similar stylistic patterns to your letters.

Tools for writing

If this is your first piece of serious writing then prepare yourself properly for the task. First of all, what are you going to write with? You could choose:-

Pen or pencil and paper

If you're not used to using a computer then choose this medium. You may find the words flow more easily if you are not faced with a blank computer screen, and it will remind you of writing a letter. At some point your writing may have to be transcribed onto a computer. Another option is to write your story straight into a permanent notebook, as long as your writing is sufficiently legible and you don't anticipate making many mistakes.

Typewriter

If you like using a typewriter, and don't want the expense of buying a computer, stick to what you know best. Use A4 sheets of paper, and write with a double space between the lines, to make editing easier afterwards. Your words may still have to be transcribed onto a computer at some point, or it may be possible to scan them in.

Computer

This is by far the most time-efficient way of working. You can either buy a word-processing programme like Microsoft Word, or use the word processing programme which comes with your computer, which should do the job comfortably. You can edit as you go along, and your words can be sent easily to a publisher or printer. You can also print draft copies for family and friends to read as you go along.

Tape recorder

One way of collecting information from someone who is unwilling or unable to write is by using a tape recorder. The advantage is that it's less tiring to talk than to write, so you'll cover a lot of ground quickly. Also, you can carry a tape recorder around with you and record at any time. Transcribing a tape, however, is very time-consuming and you, or the transcriber, will take two to three times as long to write up the words as it took to speak them. Computer software is available which can convert speech into computer text.

Are you sitting comfortably?

Next, find a suitable place to write. A good firm chair and desk may suit a fit person, but there's nothing wrong with sitting in your favourite armchair. You may land up with pieces of paper and photographs spread around you on the floor. But as long as your family (and pets!) understand this is your space you shouldn't have a problem.

If you are writing your book with someone else then make sure you are both comfortable.

How to start

As the chapter on structure pointed out, you don't have to start writing a life story with the subject's birth. In fact that's rather a boring way to start. Even the Obituaries columns in the newspapers rarely start with the person's birth (or death), but with their achievements. If you do intend to write a strictly chronological book then try to think of a more imaginative first sentence to announce your arrival in the world than by stating, "I was born on 3rd July 1946..."

How about:

"My mother liked to claim I was born within the sound of Bow Bells, although I'm not sure that you could describe me as a true Cockney. It's true that I was born at the Royal London Hospital on Whitechapel Road in the East End of London on 5th December 1939, but by the time I was five days old I had been taken home to Stoke Newington, well out of earshot of the Bow Bells."

Or:

"My birth was hardly an easy one, as my mother weighed more before she became pregnant than when she gave birth to me. However, we both survived my arrival on 24th November 1937, and I'm still here to tell the following tale."

An unusual baptism certificate could be used as illustration. It doesn't matter if it's in an aged condition

If you know the details, don't underestimate the readability of the story of your birth. It will be endlessly fascinating to immediate members of the family.

If you don't intend to start with your birth, then think of an event or thought that will grab the reader's attention. These are the first words that your audience will read (apart from the Introduction, about which more later) and you want to draw them in. Once you have chosen the subject matter, start to write it down as if you were telling a friend or writing a letter. Try to suit the language to the subject.

If you are describing a piece of action, like a race, or an accident, keep the language spare. Describe what happened clearly. After you have recounted the event, describe your reaction to it. If you start with a subject which makes you feel emotional just write your thoughts as they tumble out. Don't stop to consider whether you sound *over*-emotional. After a period of time - an hour, or a couple of days - go back and see if your words reflect what you intended to say. Such writing can be exhausting. Don't change anything if you don't need to.

CASE STUDY – JOAN'S MANUSCRIPT

Joan first began to write up the story of her disabled son, David, on holiday in Tunisia. She scribbled down a few words in a notepad, intending to continue back home.

As is often the case, she set the project to one side. David's death had affected her greatly and she didn't feel ready to write the rest of the story.

Five years later she decided to tackle the book again, to mark the 10th anniversary of David's death. But the handwritten pages had gone missing.

By now Joan had a computer, so she wrote straight into a word-processing programme. Like a good omen, her original notebook turned up while she was writing, and she was able to include those early thoughts in her book.

Joan chose to have her book printed as a paperback. She saved much time - and money - by working on a computer. But her book was made richer by including those first handwritten pages. Make sure you choose the medium that's best for you.

Perhaps you'll start with the description of a place - a house, a village or a favourite haunt. Describe the minute detail of the place so it comes alive. But be careful not to overwrite, by using too many beautiful, flowery, adjectives. Writing which is too nostalgic can also make embarrassing reading.

A few do's and don'ts of writing

Do
- type your manuscript double-spaced between the lines and leave wide margins for easy editing.
- keep your sentences reasonably short. Long, rambling sentences can be confusing for the reader.
- keep the punctuation simple. Use commas and full stops, but don't introduce too many colons or semi-colons unless you are familiar with using them. A good book on punctuation is *Eats Shoots and Leaves* by Lynne Truss, which will guide you through the hoops.
- keep paragraphs short. Each paragraph break gives the reader a breather.
- think about your vocabulary and keep a dictionary by your side. Try not to repeat words, but find an alternative. You can also use *Roget's Thesaurus.*

Don't
- use too many exclamation marks. A story which is exciting doesn't need them. You rarely see an exclamation mark in a newspaper (although some stories beggar belief).
- assume too much knowledge on the part of the reader. Remember to introduce new people in the book. When you are describing something technical use simple everyday language, rather than jargon.

Ghostwriters

A ghostwriter will write your autobiography for you. For example, David Beckham's bestseller, *My Side*, was written by the broadcaster Tom Watt. Most celebrity and sporting autobiographies are ghostwritten.

It might seem strange to suggest using a ghostwriter when this project is about writing your own life story, but you may need substantial help with aspects of the writing, or you may be too busy to write yourself.

Be aware that this service can be expensive and you're not guaranteed results. It is important to strike up a good relationship with the writer as you may be sharing personal information with him or her. Ask to see an early sample of 'your' words to make sure that they are written in a style you like.

6. Writing As a Routine

You have crossed a major hurdle by starting your book - now you need to keep going. After you have completed your first section of writing, be it a few paragraphs or a number of pages, show it to someone. Ask for an honest opinion. Does it make sense, first of all? Is it easy to read? Is it interesting? You won't need a second opinion at every stage of your writing but it's good to touch base with a reader early on, to ensure that you are heading in the right direction. You may need to explain to them how this first chapter will end if it's incomplete. Listen to their criticisms. It's far easier to adjust your writing at this stage, rather than three quarters of the way through the book.

It's also time to refer to your structure and make sure that you have included everything you intended in this first section.

Establishing a routine

You now need to carry on with your writing on a regular basis. Your personality will have some bearing on your progress. If you are a well organised person then set aside a time each day to write. Allow yourself an hour or two in the morning, afternoon, or evening - whenever you are least likely to be disturbed - and aim to write so many words a day. If, on the other hand, you tend to leave things to the last minute (like many journalists) then you may need to set yourself deadlines. Perhaps there is an anniversary or birthday on the horizon, for which you would like the finished article to be ready. Give yourself a deadline to complete the text two to three months before you need the book, so that there is adequate time for editing and printing.

Should such a date seem too remote then set a deadline in a week's time to have a particular section written. Set aside two or three evenings in the week when you will write and not be distracted by other offers of entertainment, even the television.

Try to pick the time of day to write when you are least sleepy. Personally, I have to get all my household chores done in the morning before I can settle down to write. Even then, by mid-afternoon I need some fresh air, or I doze off at the keyboard. If you are an early riser, writing for an hour or two before everyone else wakes up can be fruitful.

Length of the project

How long will it take you to write your life story? This is one of the hardest things to judge at the outset. It depends on so many factors; the amount of material you have, how quickly you write, how much time you can devote to the project. Generally - and this is based only on experience - the book will take months, rather than weeks or years to produce. This is if you are writing regularly, and assuming that editing and printing will take up to a couple of months.

You can make a project last as long as you want. If you need the book for an anniversary in three months' time then you'll be sufficiently motivated to get it written in four to six weeks, edited professionally (another two weeks), and printed in a month.

On the other hand, you may undertake some research in the course of writing the book. You may wish to find out more about your family (especially your grandparents' generation), or if your book is centred on a hobby or career you may wish to research additional background information.

If you decide to stop writing for a while, don't let your text sit idle. This is a good opportunity for a member of the family or a friend to read your work-in-progress and give you a second opinion. Reread the work yourself on a regular basis and keep referring to your structure.

Book Length
It's obvious from your bookshelves that a book can be any length. To give you an idea of various lengths here are a few statistics: this book which is relatively short contains 20,000 words; *A Year in Provence* by Peter Mayle has around 90,000 words; *Captain Corelli's Mandolin* by Louis de Bernieres 186,000; and, to put it all in perspective, the Bible contains 783,137 words.

A life story often falls between 25,000 and 60,000 words.

It can be useful to keep a tally of your words as you write, either to tell a printer at some stage, or to work out an approximate, final length.

Appearance
As your writing progresses think about how you want your book to look. Here is a list of questions to help you.

How important is its appearance to you?
Do you wish to leave the manuscript as a written or typed document or do you wish to have it printed and bound?
Do you envisage a paperback or a hardback?
Do you want to group the pictures in the middle of the book or do you want them spread throughout the text?
Do you want extra illustrative material, such as drawings or cartoons? Do you know someone who would produce them?
What look do you want for the cover - bold, understated, serious, informal?

In Chapter 10 we'll come back to these questions, but start to think about your book's appearance now, while you're writing.

Setbacks

Most of all, ask yourself the question: am I enjoying myself? If you're not, then try to analyse where your difficulty lies.

Are you finding the writing hard? Is it because you lack the vocabulary, the text just doesn't flow, or you're not very good at grammar? Sometimes, it's just best to get the facts down and worry about how it's written later. There are professional writing and editing services available.

Is the material too emotional for you to deal with? You'll have to decide if this is the right time for you to unburden yourself on paper. Maybe you should be seeking counselling rather than writing on your own, if it is bringing back a lot of painful memories.

Is it boring? Maybe you have included a few repetitive details which can be edited out later. This is certainly true of diary-writing.

Did you really need to recount what you ate for breakfast *every* day? With hindsight, just the occasional reference would have been sufficient.

Losing motivation

This is a tough one, because writing a book is such a lengthy process, compared to other jobs you set yourself, like painting a room or weeding the garden. It's also a solitary activity, so you don't have the constant encouragement or participation from work colleagues or family.

First of all, you don't *have* to write this book. For the above reasons, or any others, it's perfectly acceptable to change your mind. We've all taken up an evening class, or tried a new form of exercise, and not enjoyed it.

Don't get depressed or feel guilty that you've let people down, simply explain why this has not turned out to be the right project for you.

CASE STUDY — TERRY CHANGES HIS MIND

Terry retired at the age of 65 after a successful life in financial services. He had become rich, but soon grew bored with time on his hands. His wife and daughter both thought it would be a good idea if Terry wrote his life story.

In fact Terry had enjoyed English at school and he began to jot down his childhood memories from the Second World War. He even paid a visit to Felixstowe where he had been evacuated.

Then, a friend called Terry with an idea for a part-time business. He couldn't resist and began to spend less time on his writing. Then a charity requested his help. Of course, he agreed. As Terry wrote less, his enthusiasm for the project waned, and eventually he stopped. That was fine, because Terry was happy and occupied. But, I hope he takes up his writing again one day...

However, if you do wish to continue, but need to feel better motivated, then try to pinpoint the problem. If you decide that you need professional help with the writing you'll have to spend more money, but if it means that you complete the book, it will be worthwhile.

Also, talk to a family member or friend whose opinion you respect. Show them your writing and get some feedback. If this encourages you, perhaps you could send each chapter as you complete it to this person for their response. Feed off other people's enthusiasm.

Difficult subjects

How do you deal with sensitive issues? Many families have skeletons in the cupboard, or someone who has been through trauma, breakdown or divorce. Tread carefully, at all costs. You don't want your book to cause pain. You will have to examine the cost of telling the truth. One suggestion is to write about the particular issue and then show the text to the parties concerned. They may be less worried than you imagined, or by changing the odd word, be satisfied with the result. However, if someone objects to what you have written and you respect their opinion, you may have to say something along the lines of:

"Rob's breakdown in the late '80s led to divorce from Celia, but I respect their wishes not to give any further details about this event."

If the issue contains very personal information about someone you may have to leave it out. Remember, your book may be read by children and grandchildren of the individual.

7. More Techniques

In this chapter we will look at some techniques to make your life story a more interesting and enjoyable read. We'll then consider additional elements like chapter headings, the introduction, and an index.

Continuous prose can be relentless chapter after chapter, so here are some ways in which you can break it up.

Quotes and Extracts

This is a way of making the best use of your source material. You want your family to come alive in the book and one way is by quoting from letters and diaries. After you have described a particular event you could quote the response or feelings which you or your subject experienced. You can quote using just a single sentence or several paragraphs. If your book is based mainly on someone else's diaries then you might mix your own narrative voice with quite lengthy excerpts from the diaries. With other people's letters and diaries remember to obtain their permission to quote from them.

Speech

To describe a particular incident you can recount it as if it were in a novel, by telling the story through speech. Speech can be used for good dramatic effect, especially if important news is announced in this way.

You can convey excitement, shock or sadness with greater impact than through pure prose.

For example, in this extract, Joan, the mother, is with her

young, sick child in hospital when a doctor arrives unexpectedly, to tell her that her child can neither see nor hear:

There must have been an indication of the pain I felt on my face, because he continued, uninvited, "Don't worry, he won't live".

No further explanation is needed to convey the impact of this statement.

Visual Breaks

You will probably decide to group most of your photographs or illustrative material together in the middle of the book or, possibly, at the end of each chapter. However, you may have some  visual material which could be displayed in the text, like poems, drawings, lists or newspaper articles. You can include the item by placing it in a box, with the relevant text flowing around it. In a long, wordy chapter the reader will be grateful for the break.

When you've completed writing the main body of the text it may be tempting to give a huge sigh of relief and feel you've finished. In fact there are still a few writing tasks to perform.

Chapter Headings

The main job of the chapter heading is to tell the reader what to expect in the following pages. You could give your chapters very simple headings and dates, along the lines of 'Early Years 1942-47'. You also have the opportunity to be more creative. You could use a phrase from the chapter itself which strikes you as being apt (and still include dates if appropriate). A quotation from a poem or the Bible, or the motto for an organisation, could also be suitable.

You can play with words, so that a chapter about a keen cyclist is called 'Biking Mad'. You might also distort the title of a well-known book or poem, as in 'Three Men and a Girl in a Boat', to describe a sailing holiday.

Keep the chapter headings reasonably short, so that they fit on one line, and don't be too clever in every chapter heading, or the reader may get confused.

Introduction

These will be the first words people read. You don't have to include an introduction, especially if the first chapter gives a lot of background information. But it is a very useful way of signposting the reader through the text. Leave writing the introduction until you have finished the rest of your book. You may wish to include:

- your reasons for writing - what inspired you to write, who the book is for, what you have gained from writing it.

- an anecdote to illustrate the above or an important moment in your life. This will give colour to your prose and draw the reader in.

- if the book isn't chronological or is arranged thematically, explain how it's organised.

- acknowledgements and thanks. You may wish to thank family members, friends or professional advisors who have either helped directly during the writing of the book or supported you in some way.

The introduction can be difficult to write. You are so close to the material that it's hard to extract the key elements of the story. You hope to entice the reader to continue, but need to include some facts. The mix of explanation and 'come on' factor is a delicate balance. Show your introduction to a family member or friend and see if it fulfils these aims.

Dedication

Books are often dedicated to someone closely associated with the author. This usually appears alone on a page, near the front of the book. For example:

> To Lucie and Harry
> May this be an inspiration to you

Family tree

It is a good idea to draw up a simple family tree, showing as a minimum your generation and one either side of it. It saves you having to continually remind readers in the text of family members, and provides an 'at-a-glance' view of the family. You can of course make the family tree more detailed and if you have been researching the family's genealogy this would be an excellent outlet for it.

Place the family tree either on the inside front cover or on a page near the front of the book.

Appendices

An appendix contains additional information which is too bulky to put into the main body of the text, and is placed at the end of the book. A typical example could be a very long diary extract, covering several pages, which would have broken up the flow of the prose.

Bibliography and addresses

If you have alluded to books and organisations in the text it is useful to group publishing and contact details on a page near the back of the book. You can add any further useful books, magazines, charities or companies you think would be of interest, even if they have not been mentioned directly.

Index

This is the chore which most writers dread, and why they use professional indexers. Most life stories have no need of an index, especially if the book is to be read mainly by family and friends. An index will be useful if the book refers to numerous individuals, places, organisations and themes, and a wider audience is envisaged.

Try to think laterally, so if Auntie Joy used to be employed on fire-watching duties during the Second World War, this would appear in an index under three entries; Auntie Joy, fire watching and the war.

If you decide to compile the index yourself start by writing down the names of the individuals, themes, etc, which you wish to include in a long list, against which you will put the page numbers once the book is paginated.

Alert your printer early on if you want to include an index to make sure sufficient space is left for it.

Let's recap

At this point it's useful to refer to the following list which outlines every single page of your book, and check you have thought about each one. You may decide to leave some blank and others will be irrelevant to your project.

Front cover
Inside front cover
Title page (usually repeats the cover title, author's name and publisher if appropriate)
Copyright page (includes publishing information, your copyright as author, copyright and liability statements)
Contents page
Introduction
Acknowledgements
Dedication
Family tree
The text, divided into chapters and illustrations
Appendices
Useful addresses, bibliography
Index
Inside back cover
Back cover

8. Collective Memoirs

As Chapter 1 pointed out, collective memoirs provide a lasting way of marking the anniversary of a group. When there are many contributors it is strongly advisable to appoint an editor who will collect the contributions and assemble them.

If this job seems too much for one person, then it could be shared so that one person is responsible for gathering the information and another edits it and compiles the book.

The person who is gathering the information needs to work out the exact requirements from contributors, say, some writing of no more than 200 words and a photograph. He or she needs to be able to inspire people to take part, and to cajole them when they are late handing in the material.

For the individual who will edit and lay out the material it is very helpful to have desktop publishing (dtp) and a scanner. Material is likely to arrive written by hand, by email or be typed, accompanied by old photos and newspaper cuttings.

You could always use a professional desktop publishing firm if you don't have the equipment yourself. Even so, you will want to organise the material into some order and think about presentation. Flexibility and patience are good qualities for both these people.

Allow plenty of time for a collective memoir. It may take at least six months to request and collect all the material, and a further six months to get it edited and printed.

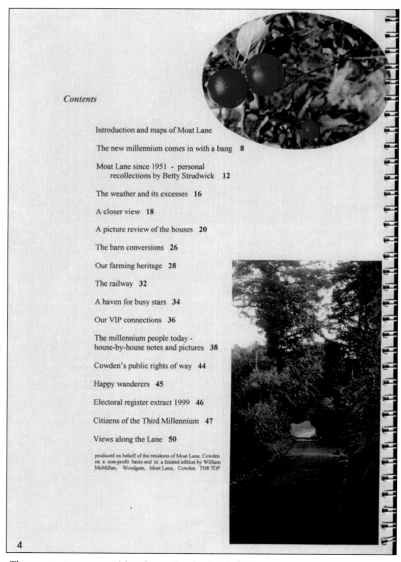

Contents

Introduction and maps of Moat Lane

The new millennium comes in with a bang 8

Moat Lane since 1951 - personal
    recollections by Betty Strudwick 12

The weather and its excesses 16

A closer view 18

A picture review of the houses 20

The barn conversions 26

Our farming heritage 28

The railway 32

A haven for busy stars 34

Our VIP connections 36

The millennium people today -
house-by-house notes and pictures 38

Cowden's public rights of way 44

Happy wanderers 45

Electoral register extract 1999 46

Citizens of the Third Millennium 47

Views along the Lane 50

produced on behalf of the residents of Moat Lane, Cowden
on a non-profit basis and in a limited edition by William
McMillan, Woodgate, Moat Lane, Cowden TN8 7DP

4

The contents page to *Moat Lane, Cowden 2000*. Make your contents page more
visually interesting than in a conventional book

Here's a step-by-step guide to getting the job done.

1. Hold a meeting or talk to as many people as possible in the group to ensure there is support for the project. Talk through the idea with a printer so that you can tell people the approximate cost of a single copy.
2. Appoint one or two individuals to oversee it.
3. Decide the contents of the book in broad terms - anecdotes, pictures, an overall introduction, historical documents, a map.
4. Work out very specific requirements from contributors.
5. Give contributors these requirements and set a deadline.
6. Start to make decisions about the size of the book and its appearance.
7. Collect the material and check it's what you asked for. Chase late contributors.
8. Once the material is in, talk again to the printer, tell him how you will get him the book (in its raw state, typeset, or with pages laid out), and how many copies you will want. Get an exact price.
9. Depending on the technology available to you prepare the material. Seek advance orders for copies.
10. Follow one of the following printing options:- a) print it yourself using dtp, b) use dtp to do the page layouts, but take it to a print shop to be printed and bound, c) send all the material to a commercial printer for printing and binding.
11. Advertise the book to the target audience.
12. Hold a book launch party.

9. Editing Your Manuscript

Professional writers need editors and, at some point, so may you. An editor's function is to make sure that the story makes sense, that it is well written, and that it isn't libellous. There may also be copyright questions.

A manuscript which is to be privately published may not need to be edited to the same extent as a commercial book. Consider the following questions:

1. Will your book be read just by family and close friends? You will not require a professional editor but you could ask a member of your family or a friend to read the text to ensure that it makes sense and to pick up spelling and grammatical errors. It's amazing how a fresh pair of eyes will spot mistakes that you missed. You should also reread the entire text yourself and be prepared to make changes.

If you are considering having your book printed and have hand-written or typed your manuscript, it's time to get it transcribed onto a computer - it's faster and easier to edit this way. You can reread the text yourself in its original form if you prefer, but make sure that any changes are added to the computerised version.

2. Does your book read well? If not, then a professional editor will be invaluable, for he or she can reword clumsy phrases, re-organise the material and make suggestions about pictures and layout. An editor can even work with you while you write the book, not just amend your words afterwards.

3. Is there any contentious material? You may need to get your manuscript read by a lawyer, even if it is purely for private publication. Such material might include the outcome of a court case (the terms of a final settlement may be bound by a confidentiality clause), or any accusations made against an individual or organisation.

4. Is any material taken from another source, such as a poem, a drawing, or a quotation, and therefore subject to copyright law? In particular be careful about downloading information from the internet without checking the copyright. If your book is for private publication, especially if you can prove an educational or non-profit making purpose, copyright is often given free. An acknowledgement of the source of the material may suffice and these usually appear on the copyright page near the front of the book. A commercial publisher will deal with copyright issues in-house.

If either you or a friend decide to edit the book then bear in mind the following considerations.

Style, grammar, spelling
While it is hoped that you will have some feedback from family and friends who have read sections of the book, go through the text with a toothcomb for errors. Almost inevitably some will get through, and many commercially published books are printed with a few mistakes. Use the spell-check facility on your computer.

Content and material
Make sure that you have included everything you intended. Look through your structure and original materials again. When you discover you have missed something out return to the rele-

vant section and see if you can jiggle the text to fit it in. If you can't consider including the material in an appendix.

Also take this opportunity to remove, or reduce in length, sections of the text. At this stage editing often means cutting the text rather than expanding it. Be fairly hard on yourself - better to be concise than a waffler.

Overall shape

Once you have reread the text make sure that the book is balanced structurally. For example, if you experienced your greatest achievements in your twenties, make sure that this is reflected in the balance of the book.

It's unlikely that you'll get this far and decide to restructure radically, especially if your text runs chronologically.

If these tasks seems overwhelming you may need an external editor. Look on the internet for companies who offer self-publishing services. This is a growth area and there are now a number of companies offering idea-to-publication services including, writing, editing and printing. More information about self-publishers is given in Chapter 11.

10. A Good-Looking Book

The appearance of your book will say a lot about you as a person. Your choices may also be influenced by cost. First, how important is your book's appearance to you? The following options may help you define your ideas.

Leather-bound

If you want one or two high-quality copies of your book go to a company which binds university theses. The material used may be buckram and the pages (usually A4) are stitched. The cover will show the title and your name, embossed in gold, which will be repeated on the spine. This service costs around £40 per copy. Ask for the name of a recommended binder from your nearest university.

Hardback

This is the most expensive option and, if you're really looking to the long-term, the most durable. If you have very strong illustrative material you may decide that it will be best displayed in a hardback, which will also look good on your coffee table.

It may also be the most suitable format for an anniversary present or if the subject has an important position in public life. Children's books are often produced in hardback so that they will last. Do you have any such requirements? If your book is to be kept in a public place, like a village hall or community centre, then a hardback may be the most practical option. Bear in mind that a printer may charge upwards of £25 a copy (for 50 to 100 copies).

Paperback

A popular choice. A paperback feels like a *real* book. It's flexible, durable, can incorporate text and pictures, is easy to post, and people can keep it on their shelves along with the rest of their books. A paperback feels more informal than a hardback. Digital printing has brought self-published paperbacks within reach of many people's pockets, and a 100-page book may cost around £10 to £15 a copy to print (for 50 to 100 copies).

The costs for hardbacks and paperbacks may go down if you print more copies.

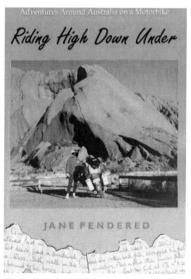 

Both these books were self-published as paperbacks

Spiral-bound

This format has an even more informal look and is not as durable as the above formats. Its advantage is that you can produce quite a large book, say up to 250 pages, on A4 paper, at a reasonably low cost. If you are considering a collective memoir (say the history of a village, with lots of photographs), it's also a flexible format with a scrapbook feel, easy to dip in and out. Costs per copy at a High Street print shop may be £5 or less.

Stapled

This is an inexpensive option and, strictly speaking, you will end up with a booklet rather than a book. Size is limited by the strength of the staples and these are likely to rust or break over time. That said, if your book is short and you wish to circulate it widely (and keep postage costs down), this is a quick, short-term option. A stapled, 50-page book will cost well under £5 per copy at a High Street print shop.

Ring-bound

This is the least expensive and easiest option. A ring binder from a stationer costs £2-3, into which your written or typed pages can be inserted. Photocopy your pages, double-sided preferably, and make as many copies of your book as you like. You can protect the first and last pages with sheets of clear perspex.

Style

A related area to consider is the visual style of the book. Just as you might plan a party as a 'black tie' or 'smart casual' event, you need to choose a look for your book. This is influenced by a number of factors.

Covers

Books have four covers, outside front and back covers, and inside front and back covers.

The outside front cover will comprise the title of the book, possibly a sub-title, the name of the author and some kind of illustration (e.g. a photograph) or design. How do you want the cover to appear? Bold, formal, glitzy, serious? Think of adjectives to describe the look you want.

The outside back cover may carry another illustration, and the 'blurb' - a short description of the book to attract the reader.

The inside front cover may be left blank, or can be used for an illustration such as a map, a family tree, or a portrait of the subject.

The inside back cover may also be left blank or you might include a short author's biography and an up-to-date picture.

Visually, it's good to leave either the inside front or back cover blank, so that the book doesn't seem overcrowded to the reader. Occasional white spaces let the book 'breathe'.

Cover typeface
There are hundreds of typefaces from which to choose. You may leave this decision to a printer, but look at the difference in the typefaces below, used for book titles on front covers.

The first is Arial, a favourite in many business documents because it is clear and unfussy. The second is Freescript and is suitable for an informal memoir. The third is Lucida Calligraphy, a semi-formal type with a few flourishes, and the fourth Vivaldi, a flamboyant typeface suitable for someone who is creative and artistic.

1. A History of J. Taylor & Sons

2. *My Gap Year in South America*

3. *A Rural Life in the 1950s*

4. *Following in the Footsteps of the Poets*

With desktop publishing all these options are open to you. A printer may have even more. The title of this book and the text are printed in Book Antiqua, a typeface I like for its elegant lines and because, like Arial, it's easy on the eye in solid text.

Other popular text typefaces include Times New Roman and Gill Sans MT.

If you want to print a poem you could use the same typeface as your text, or use a contrasting one such as Century, an old-fashioned looking type, seen below.

Thou still unravished bride of quietness,
Thou fosterchild of Silence and slow Time,
(From *Ode on a Grecian Urn* by John Keats)

Paper

Think of the paper used in newspapers and then of the glossy paper in an art book. Choose a suitable paper for your memoir. Take a look at the books on your shelves and get a broad idea of the kind of paper you like. There are also speciality papers available if you want an 'aged' look, for example.

Bear in mind the heavier the paper the higher the postage costs. Paper which is used in offices for photocopying weighs 80grams per square metre (gsm). A slightly heavier paper, maybe 90gsm or even 100gsm, is ideal for a life story, and photographs also reproduce well.

Another option is to use a lighter paper, e.g. 70gsm for the text, and a glossy, heavier paper for the photographs. This, though attractive, may work out more expensively as the photographs will have to be printed separately to the text.

Text style

Apart from typeface design and paper you will need to decide how to arrange and present all the material, both text and illustrative. Consider for the moment elements relating to the text. How much text do you want on each page? Look at your bookshelves again and see what a difference the size of the typeface, the width of the margins and the line spacing, make. For example, old paperbacks have small typefaces and narrow margins so that more words fit onto the page. In other words, the books were smaller and, therefore, cheaper to produce. Nowadays, paperbacks are bigger, use a larger typeface and have wider margins. They are easier to read as a result.

You will also need to make style decisions for the chapter headings, sub-headings, diary extracts, and so forth. Again, you need to look at typeface, size and position on the page.

If you have desktop publishing (dtp) then you can experiment at home, if not discuss the options with your printer. Dtp is further considered in Chapter 11.

Picking your pictures

In a life story, illustration is more important than it is in most other books. Your family and friends will wish to see photographs of you as much as they will want to read the book. You can include as many pictures as you like and, because of digital printing technology, the book will be no more expensive. A life story of about 100 pages might well have 30 to 40 photographs accompanying it.

Photographs are likely to be the predominant form of illustration. Once you start looking through your albums it's surprising how quickly you assemble a pile of pictures. Try to get a balanced selection between different periods of your life.

Don't worry too much about their quality. Digital technology can sometimes rescue a very poor picture.

Obviously the higher the quality of the original the better the finished outcome, and any particularly good pictures can be given prominence on the page.

The most common way to display pictures is in either one or two sections in the middle of the book. If you look at a few biographies you can get an idea of how your pictures might be arranged, usually between one and four on a page, with captions. Pictures used to be organised like this because they were printed on a different paper to the text, but they do carry impact when grouped together.

It is just as acceptable for pictures to be placed either at the end of each chapter or within the text. The only additional cost will be in time taken to lay out the pages. The more the text is interrupted by pictures the longer the design takes. This format may also feel unfamiliar to the reader used to a conventional layout.

Illustrations other than photographs may include drawings (e.g. portraits), newspaper articles or poems. Treat these as if they were photographs, placing them in their chronological sequence. The printer will be able to scan them in just like photos. At the end of this chapter some sample pages of photographs are shown.

Captions

Place all the pictures in the order in which you would like them to appear and number them on the back in pencil. Now you need to write a caption for each picture, numbering each caption to match the picture. Captions should be fairly short, e.g.. 'Johnny at the fair in Scarborough in 1966'. If there is more than one person in a picture, make sure you include a *left* or *right* in the caption, e.g. 'Johnny, *left*, and mother, at the fair in Scarborough in 1966'. With a group of people, add a '*From left*, Johnny, Helen, etc'. Captions should be clear and explanatory, even witty if you want. Type out the numbered captions on a separate piece of paper. Keep your pictures and captions together as this is where mistakes are likely to creep in.

Cover pictures

When you are looking through your pictures pick a couple for the front and back covers. In a life story it's important to display the subject on the front. The picture for the cover is the most important one in the whole book. You may have a favourite picture, but if not, then choose one which shows the subject in a typical situation, not necessarily a formal portrait which might look rather stuffy. Bear in mind that the picture does not have to fill the entire area of the front page. You need room for the title, maybe a sub-title and the author's name. For this reason the central image has to be a strong one.

Choose a second picture for the back cover. Perhaps this time the subject could be with someone else, or if a building or activity plays an important part in the book, use an image of it. Your front and back cover pictures may be repeated in your picture sections inside if you particularly like them.

A pictorial record

Your pictures will need to be interesting and also of good technical quality. In a 100-page book you could include up to 300 pictures. Select a good balance of pictures from throughout your life and try not leave out any family members. Exceptionally good pictures could appear on a page of their own, while slightly inferior ones could be presented in a group of four on a page. By keeping them small you will disguise their poorer quality.

You should probably choose a large format such as A4 or slightly smaller to show off your pictures to best advantage. The book can still be bound by any of the given methods.

Greater emphasis will be placed on the captions, as they are going to have to tell the story. Give lots of detail about the people in each picture, as well as where and when it was taken. It's not enough just to name names. Arrange the pictures in order, numbered on the back in pencil, along with the numbered captions, as explained above.

If you want to produce your pictorial record at home you will need a good scanner and a photo editing programme like Adobe Photoshop. You can get rid of unwanted shadows, sharpen up the focus, and crop (trim) the pictures, adding any number of special effects. If you enjoy photography then this can be a very rewarding project.

If you don't want to invest in this technology then a commercial printer will be able to do the job for you. You can place a piece of tracing paper over the picture and mark any areas you want cropped out. Secure the tracing paper with a paper clip or masking tape. You can also point out where you would like dust spots removed or someone's face lightened.

You can use other kinds of illustrative material in a pictorial record. Portraits, maps and line drawings are a few examples. If you can scan the material you can include it. Even memorabilia like theatre or sports programmes, ration books or old passports with their stamps can bring past events to life.

A selection of old family portraits

Alice Moyce c.1890

Betty, Robert and Gordon
Foster in the 1920s

Winifred Openshaw c.1900

Ann Openshaw c.1880

Portrait photography becomes more informal

Vivienne and Gordon in the 1940s

Magnus, *left*,
Allegra,
Miranda and
Imogen 2003

©Mel Smith

Panoramic pictures can fill the whole page to dramatic effect

(from *Riding High Down Under*)

Colour snaps of people and places

In the French Alps 2004:
top: walking in the mountains above Valmorel
bottom left: mountain biking
bottom right: watching the professionals as the Tour de France passes through the Col de la Madeleine

Pets are important family members too

Left: Charlie, famed for catching fish

Bottom left: Mr Pip, a remarkable dog who lived to 18 years
Bottom right: Algernon

At Home

The author's great-grandparents bought this homestead in Ontario, Canada in the late 19th century

How that barn turned into this comfortable dwelling... the last 20 years have seen many farm building conversions   (from *Moat Lane 2000*)

A barbeque at home with family and friends

11. Publishing and Printing Options

Publishing and printing technologies have changed substantially in recent years and the advent of desktop publishing (dtp) and digital printing have brought self-publishing within the reach of many people.

Dtp allows you to produce much of your book on a computer, where previously you would have needed a typewriter, a typesetter and a page designer. You can now write, edit, typeset, design and lay out pages, and scan in the pictures, all from home. You will need a computer, a printer and a scanner. If you already have these pieces of equipment then you are well on the way to being able to self-publish your book.

If you would like to learn about dtp as part of this project then you are going to need to buy a desktop publishing programme. For PCs you could try Microsoft Publisher and for Apple Macs you can buy Quark Express. Local education authorities and the London College of Printing run courses in dtp.

This book doesn't attempt to give you technical instructions as individual publishing programmes vary. You may still decide to get the book bound professionally.

Unless you have these items, think carefully about how much you want to invest in technology before you make a purchase.

Let's recap
At this point your manuscript is written and edited, and your pictures chosen and captioned. You now have to put these different elements together and finish your book. In the previous chapter we looked at production options (e.g. paperback or

hardback) and gave some thought to style elements such as typefaces. Now it's time to make these choices. Decide how many copies you want and set a budget.

Typesetting

If you're using dtp you will have plenty of typefaces from which to choose. If not, then ask a printer for guidance.

Printing and binding

These two processes often go together. There are different kinds of printer. Many towns have High Street print-shops, which will print, then spiral-bind or staple your book. This option is suitable for straight-forward printing projects. If you are using dtp take in the pages, already typeset and laid-out for printing.

Commercial printers will be able to undertake the above and also take on more complicated books, where there are a lot of photographs within the text, or graphics. If you wish to have a paperback or hardback book you will need to go to a commercial printer. Seek a personal recommendation where possible or look in Yellow Pages. Obtain three quotes as you would for other work.

Opting for a self-publishing company

If you are unwilling or unable to make the above choices then you could go to a self-publisher.

These companies are aimed at people who wish to privately produce a book for family and friends. Print runs are often low (as few as 50 copies is common) and, as we've said, the project is akin to having a family photograph taken. You pay for the publishing and printing service, but distribute the book yourself.

Self-publishers will offer services through from writing to binding, along with a high degree of personal involvement. For the more technical aspects of publishing, especially typesetting, printing and binding, a self-publisher can guide you through the hoops.

Services are often charged individually. Make sure that you are aware of these charges when you first talk to a self-publisher. You can find such companies on the internet and through personal recommendation.

What will it cost?

The cost of self-publishing a life story can vary hugely. Because you may be printing a small number of copies (compared to a commercial printing run of several thousand), the costs per copy can seem quite high. It may be that giving the books as birthday or Christmas presents helps justify the expenditure.

As has been suggested you can simply put your hand-written or typed pages into a ring binder for less than £5. At the other end of the scale, you can spend up to £5,000 on a very stylish hardback or leather-bound volume, employing professional help along the way. Bear in mind that the costs may seem high now, but your book will last for generations.

Number of copies

Make a list of all family members and friends to whom you would like to give a copy. Add a few extra, as cousins, distant relatives and old friends may request a copy a year or two after initial publication. Also, don't forget the grandchildren.

Now think of any group of people who might be prepared to pay for the book and where you could at least cover your costs. This might include local organisations, interest or hobby groups. You could also ask your local library to stock a couple of copies.

If you opt for digital publishing you will be able to re-order small quantities of your book at the same price as your first print-run (allowing for rising costs and inflation).

Publication

The hard work is over and the book paid for. The time has arrived to hold a launch party and give the book to family and friends. You might even find the time to reread it yourself at some point. Enjoy yourself.

CASE STUDY – BILL'S PRINT RUN GROWS

Bill had lived abroad for much of his life. He had joined an oil company when he was 19, at the end of the Second World War, and had spent the subsequent years in Egypt, Nigeria and South Africa. He had kept a diary of sorts, jotting down anecdotes about colleagues and encounters with the locals.

When he decided to write his memoirs, after retirement back in England, he envisaged producing a handful of copies for his family, and one or two close friends. He photocopied his pages and put them in a smart ring binder. But, Bill's anecdotes travelled well, and his tales of expat life reached the ears of former colleagues. In the end, Bill produced 100 copies of his book in hardback, at a cost of about £20 a copy. His friends were happy to pay for a memoir which captured a part of their lives, not just Bill's.

---

12. Should I sell my book?

This information is included should you want to sell a few extra copies of your book in your local area or to a specific audience. Remember to exercise caution.

ISBN number

You can obtain an International Standard Book Number (ISBN) for your book, although you are not legally required to. This is the long number and bar code on the back of a book which allows it to be ordered by bookshops. It is obtained from J. Whitaker and Sons, whose address is listed in the bibliography.

You will have to provide six copies of your book, which will be placed in the British Library and others. The service costs £77.50 for which you receive 10 ISBN numbers. As you may only publish one volume it's highly unlikely you will want to spend this amount of money. You may name yourself as publisher and bookshops will contact you if they want to order copies of your book. However, unless your book receives considerable publicity don't get your hopes up.

A Local Audience

In the first instance, your book may find an audience in your local area. You could contact bookshops to see if they would be interested in ordering any copies. To promote your book further you could try to get it reviewed by your local newspaper. Send a copy of the book and a covering letter to the reporter responsible for your area.

If local people and places are mentioned it's quite possible that the paper would be interested in doing a short profile of you. Remember to ask the paper to include details of how to obtain the book and the price.

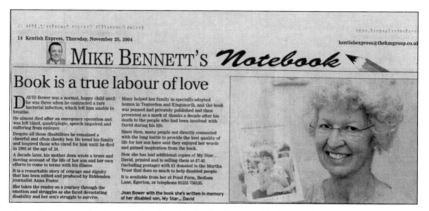

Joan Bower received some local publicity in the *Kentish Express* for her book *My Star... David*

A Wider Audience

If your book is about a particular interest or hobby you might be able to persuade a magazine to either interview you or carry an excerpt from the book. Again, write a covering letter, enclose a copy and highlight the best bits. Journalists are busy and may not have time to read the whole book. A magazine will also be interested in good photographs to illustrate the piece. Don't enclose originals of pictures at this stage but mention them in your covering letter.

If you have hopes of an even wider audience be careful. Don't commit a large sum of money to publishing the book before you receive solid orders. You are straying into vanity publishing here. If your book really is commercially viable look for a respectable publisher.

71

Price

You must price your book competitively if you hope to sell it in bookshops. Paperbacks are often priced between £6 and £10 so use this as a guide. Bear in mind that your production costs may exceed this figure and therefore not make it viable to sell. If you want to sell a small number of copies to a target audience then you may be able to charge more. A history of your village or street could be priced between £15 and £20.

Don't raise your expectations of selling your book too high. It could detract from the enjoyment of writing it if sales don't go well. Family and friends may well praise your book but they are predisposed to like it. A stranger is likely to be more critical.

If you enjoyed this project you could decide to help someone else write their memoirs. You could also set up a life story writing class with friends. Or you could just feel satisfied that you have left a legacy which your descendants will be enjoying for a long time to come.

Bibliography and addresses

Books
Writers' and Artists' Yearbook, A. & C. Black
The Writer's Handbook, Macmillan
Eats Shoots and Leaves, Lynne Truss, Profile Books

Websites
www.friendsreunited.co.uk

Addresses
London College of Printing, Elephant & Castle, London SE1 6SB.
Tel: 020 7514 6000
J. Whitaker & Sons Ltd, The Standard Book Numbering Agency,
12 Dyott Street, London WC1A 1DF.
Tel: 020 7420 6008
Website: *www.whitaker.co.uk*
YouByYou Books, Swallow Court, Dashmonden Lane,
Biddenden, Kent, TN27 8BD.
Tel: 01580 291965
Email: info@youbyyou.co.uk
Website: *www.youbyyou.co.uk*

The Author

Anna Foster has been a journalist and writer for more than 20 years. She edited *Management Today* magazine and was business editor of *The European* newspaper. She has worked as a freelance journalist for *The Times, The Telegraph* and *The Independent* newspapers.

She now runs YouByYou Books, a self-publishing company which helps people write and produce their life stories.

Anna lives in Kent with her husband and children.

©Mel Smith

About *Your Life*

This book was written on a Compaq Presario PC, using Microsoft Word and Publisher. The typeface is Book Antiqua. The photographs and illustrative material were scanned on an Epson 2400 Photo scanner and edited in Adobe Photoshop and Microsoft Publisher. The pages were typeset and laid out at YouByYou Books. The book was printed digitally by the Friary Press.